A 60-DAY DEVOTIONAL FOR THE
WOUNDED AND WEARY

RUFFLED AND REDEEMED

TAMI NIES

Copyright © 2025 by Tami Nies

ISBN Softcover: 978-1-7379112-3-4
Ebook ISBN: 978-1-7379112-7-2

All rights reserved. No part of this book may be reproduced or transmitted in any form or by any means, electronic or mechanical, including photocopying, recording or by any information storage and retrieval system, without permission in writing from the copyright owner. For information on distribution rights, royalties, derivative works or licensing opportunities on behalf of this content or work, please contact the publisher at the address below.

Printed in the United States of America.
Cover and Interior Design: Saheran Shoukat
Editor: Jessica Sommerfield

Although the author and publisher have made every effort to ensure that the information and advice in this book was correct and accurate at press time, the author and publisher do not assume and hereby disclaim any liability to any party for any loss, damage, or disruption caused from acting upon the information in this book or by errors or omissions, whether such errors or omissions result from
negligence, accident, or any other cause.

313 Publishing | 6956. Broad St, #177, Columbus, OH 43213

Scripture References

Unless otherwise noted, Scripture quotations are from various translations.
Scripture quotations marked AMP are taken from the Amplified® Bible (AMP), Copyright © 1954, 1958, 1962, 1964, 1965, 1987 by The Lockman Foundation, La Habra, CA 90631. Used by permission. All rights reserved.

Scripture quotations marked CSB have been taken from the Christian Standard Bible®, Copyright © 2017 by Holman Bible Publishers. Used by permission. Christian Standard Bible® and CSB® are federally registered trademarks of Holman Bible Publishers.

Scripture quotations marked ESV are from The Holy Bible, English Standard Version®, copyright © 2001 by Crossway, a publishing ministry of Good News Publishers. Used by permission. All rights reserved.

Scripture quotations marked KJV are from the King James Version. Public domain.

Voice – Scripture taken from The Voice™. Copyright © 2012 by Ecclesia Bible Society; published by Thomas Nelson, Inc. Used by permission. All rights reserved.

Scripture quotations marked NASB are taken from the New American Standard Bible®, Copyright © [edition year] by The Lockman Foundation. Used by permission. All rights reserved.

Scripture quotations marked NIV are taken from the Holy Bible, New International Version®. Copyright © 1973, 1978, 1984, 2011 by Biblica, Inc.™ Used by permission. All rights reserved worldwide.

Scripture quotations marked NKJV are from the New King James Version®. Copyright © 1982 by Thomas Nelson. Used by permission. All rights reserved.

Scripture quotations marked NLT are taken from the Holy Bible, New Living Translation, copyright © 1996, 2004, 2015 by Tyndale House Foundation. Used by permission of Tyndale House Publishers, Inc., Carol Stream, Illinois 60188. All rights reserved.

Scripture quotations marked NLV are taken from the New Life Version, Copyright © 1969, 2003 by Barbour Publishing, Inc., Uhrichsville, Ohio. Used by permission.

Let the redeemed of the Lord say so.

Psalm 107.2 KJV

INTRODUCTION

This book shares part of my journey—a journey of reflection, loss, gratitude, and growth. I hope it will encourage you to reflect and embrace yours. This book shares a desire for more meaning and substance in life. I ached for a deeper understanding of God and a connection to Him that would spark electricity and energy in my spirit—energy as power to grow and develop completely into the being He created me to be.

Have you ever prayed, "God, what am I supposed to do? Who am I supposed to be?" Lackluster existence is not enough, is it?

Ever felt like a loser with a capital L on your forehead? Ever experienced feelings of inadequacy and self-doubt? I certainly have. But you realize this is not true, right? No matter what life looks like, no matter the negativity projected toward you and what you see, there is more to you. There was a time when the "fight" was not there. It was deep inside, buried under the muck, and I could not feel the will or the determination to fight. I could not and did not want to harness it. I am not lazy by nature. I enjoy working, creating, serving, and giving. However, circumstances can leave us depleted, less inclined to engage, and cause a do-not-care, complacent, self-deprecating attitude to manifest. I was in denial. I wore a smile in social settings, but I had failed. My irreparable first marriage and broken relationship with my offspring had yielded a "turn off the ventilator" attitude. I never thought that would happen, never. Life is unpredictable, and hindsight is 20/20. My first marriage was not on solid ground or built on a foundation to endure. Our perspectives did not synchronize. We tried, but life together was not meant to be.

So, what do we do? Acknowledgment is the first step. We cannot change or move forward until what has happened is acknowledged. Ignorance is not always bliss. We must learn, lean forward, and look ahead. Admitting failure is difficult but necessary.

I failed. There—I said it. I failed. Lack of communication and selfishness had disintegrated my marriage's stability like hail damage: it is not always noticeable, but left untreated, it leads to destruction.

What do you need to look square in the eye and own? Go ahead, look in the mirror. There is no judgment. Acknowledgement, check. Release your failures and flaws before God.

What is next? Prayer—conversation with God to share what is on your heart. Saying this aloud and crying out to God may help: "I need help. I need my energy and mojo back." Lift prayer and repentance to the omniscient and omnipotent God. He is the One who does not harbor animosity, pettiness, or loathsome characteristics. Psalm 103:9 says, "He will not always accuse, nor will he harbor his anger forever" (NIV). We repent and ask forgiveness for wrongdoing. We can lay it down at the foot of the cross and leave it there. The enemy is a LIAR! Should I repeat that? God forgives us so we can forgive ourselves. Others may choose to rehash our past deficiencies and exhibit a lack of grace, but that is not God's will. You do not carry the burden. It is okay to bow out gracefully. (Well, men bow and ladies curtsy.)

Inadequacy and lackluster existence were my mindset when this writing began. I have since redirected my focus to reflection and transformation. Reflection and repentance characterize a heart desiring to please God. The wrong decisions, errors in judgment, mistakes, intentional and deliberate actions rooted in anger, insecurity, and immaturity must all be confessed and exposed to the Creator of the universe.

No one is perfect, but that cannot be an excuse to live away from the will of God. I know right from wrong. Chances are you do, too. Yet, we justify our behavior by stating the obvious—"I'm not perfect"—and continuing a path away from the God who longs to lead us. Denial is not a defense, and neither is putting your head in the sand. Exposure subjects us to vulnerability. Vulnerability strips away our ability to pretend. We come face to face with ourselves.

Repentance can occur. We can move forward.

However, moving forward is not always lightning fast. Sometimes, it is as slow as a tortoise, but forward progression is forward progression. I am not moving lightning fast, but I am moving forward. Are you? What steps (big or small) are you taking to move forward? Make a list. I need a plan of action because I am aimless without it: a hiker without a compass, a ship's captain without a course, a pilot without a flight plan. Without direction, a successful journey is in jeopardy.

So far, you have heard a twinge of my pain and sorrow. Over the span of two years, I lost my father, grandmother, brother, and a dear friend. Each was filled with faith and will be forever bound in God's glory. Therefore, the joy of life everlasting overshadows my sorrow. I can say that no matter what comes, joy still fills me because I know where my help comes from. What does that mean? Joy is internal. It does not come from others. It is not dependent on acceptance or any external factor. My joy comes from God. My joy comes from knowing He is everywhere and in everything. Knowing that adversity, despair, and pain are not in vain. Knowing failure is not insurmountable.

Arduous work is necessary to acknowledge shortcomings. We must stand in front of the mirror and truly see what is in front of us (1 Corinthians 13:12). See the good (better qualities), see the bad (opportunities for improvement), and see the ugly (what needs transformation). When was the last time you took a good look at yourself? Not a superficial glance as you head out to an event, meeting, or date, but a time you stood in front of the mirror and really looked at yourself. Try it. What do you see? Who is looking back at you? Do you see strength, courage, fear, deceit, hatred, love, contempt, failure, or success? Is kindness present? Is there self-control? Is there patience? Is there goodness?

Life gives us various situations—good, bad, and ugly—and those situations manifest within us. We can bury them, deny them, or face them. Looking in the mirror helps us to face them. Embrace the good; be thankful. Accept the bad and glean from its presence. And the ugly? Barrel through it and transform it to beauty.

As I look in the mirror, I see signs of aging. Life and time are creating crevices. The elasticity needs a bounce back (as do I). But signs of aging are not necessarily terrible things. Aging gracefully can be appealing. After all, beauty is in the eye of the beholder. Oscar Wilde said, "With age comes wisdom, but sometimes age comes alone." Do you see wisdom in your mirror and not just signs of aging? Seeing yourself is seeing who you are. Seeing who you are helps you see who you can become. It helps you find balance in the components and transform what is less desirable into a better human being. Authenticity allows us to move in a favorable direction when harnessed with accountability. I wish to be authentic and accountable. I do not want age to come alone. Disclaimer: no one said it would be easy!

If you have continued to read, I hope it has been worth the time. I am not sure where this is going yet, but we will find out together. I will say that writing, praying, and releasing are cathartic. It has allowed me to remove what is not affirming and replace it with the life-giving sustenance of God's love so I can move and grow forward. I pray this devotional placed on my heart will allow you to acknowledge past hurts, release what holds you captive, and begin to move forward in the grace and peace of God. Love, loss, and reflection are not sequential. Failure and disappointment come amid love, loss, joy, and grief. Jubilations and tribulations intertwine. This is only the beginning, a first step. Shall we take a step together?

Take this opportunity to pray, communicate with God, and reflect on your life decisions. Open your heart to the possibilities that lie ahead and spend time connecting your heart with the God who makes all things possible. Reflect, think, write, laugh, cry, and realize every instance has brought you to this moment (Esther 4:14). Now is the time to seek and receive the presence of God—presence and power that can catapult you to the next level.

Use this devotional as a tool to reference repeatedly. Highlight and write in the margins. Express your thoughts, whatever they may be. Pray bold prayers and discover who you are. Discover who God is. We cannot know enough of His goodness, grace, and mercy. See your evolution as you capture a glimpse of mine.

DAY 1

JUST FOR ME

He died for all, that those who live should live no longer for themselves, but for Him who died for them and rose again.

– 2 Corinthians 5:15 NKJV

I intentionally focused on Good Friday as a day of reflection. It was an extraordinary Holy Week. I read Easter devotions and relived moments of photos taken at the Sea of Galilee, the Via Dolorosa, and Jerusalem. I reminisced prayer time in the Garden of Gethsemane, unable to imagine the weight Jesus carried. Weight carried just for me. I had seen and felt the power of God moving during this Holy Week. He had answered my prayers for new life, and I was overwhelmed by the love of God. Love that comes only from God.

He gave His one and only Son that we might have life (John 3:16). It is incomprehensible that God, the Father, endured the agony of His Son, a King, for you and me. Jesus endured ridicule, suffering, and torturous death on a cross, all so that we might live! (John 10:10). The victory has been won. Jesus is the Author and Finisher of our faith (Hebrews 12:2). The path is set. Jesus' life, death, and resurrection showed everyone what faith in God is. We have life because of Jesus' sacrifice. And remembering His sacrifice for us should be more than an Easter ritual.

Take a moment and remember the agony of Good Friday, the silence of Holy Saturday, and the glory of Resurrection Sunday.

---- **PRAY** ----

Thank you, God,
for Your boundless love...just for me.

DAY 2

DARKNESS SUCCUMBS

The light shines in the darkness, and the darkness has not overcome it.

– John 1:5 NIV

During an early morning drive, I realized how quickly the sky transforms from darkness to light. The darkness had succumbed to a bright sky. It reminded me that our dark moments can change quickly as well. Darkness will never overshadow light. When darkness comes, light follows. There is a Light that never dims.

I have seen God transform my darkness of failure and loss. He will do the same for you. He takes a dimly lit heart and existence and breathes in His Spirit. God illuminates every crevice. Darkness flees.

What darkness have you seen transformed into light?

Offer this verse up to Heaven: "You, LORD, keep my lamp burning; my God turns my darkness into light." (Psalm 18:28 NIV)

PRAY

God of Light, illuminate my heart; illuminate my life. In Jesus' name, amen.

DAY 3

GOOD GRIEF

The LORD is close to the brokenhearted and saves those who are crushed in spirit.

– Psalm 34:18 NIV

Unlike the Peanuts character Charlie Brown's expression of frustration, the "good grief" referenced here expresses the meaningfulness of good grieving—allowing ourselves to feel and process grief while maintaining hope.

I recently attended a beautiful and meaningful funeral mass for an old friend's parent. The cathedral was beautiful, and the priest's vestments caught my attention. When I sat in the pew, I felt my heart sink in unison with my body. Mild smoke hung in front of me. As the altar incense rose toward heaven, I prayed that my praise and petitions would rise. I bid farewell to things ending and received hope for the future.

Are you grieving anything? Grieving the loss of a loved one, the loss of a relationship or marriage, the loss of a dream, the loss of power, the loss of a home or occupation? If so, grieve and process loss. But do so in hope. Abound in it. God gives us hope for tomorrow and the future (Romans 15:13), hope for restoration and healing. Loss is devastating, crippling, and debilitating if we do not have hope. Speaking of hope, God has shown His love in providing hope in unexpected ways. No matter where you are, remain in faith. Cling to the Word of God. His promises are TRUE. He will breathe new life.

Although sadness and grief filled the cathedral, I chose a moment of "good grief" to allow the incense to lift my burden of loss. Have you experienced any moments of "good grief"?

PRAY

Loving Father, meet me where I am. Help me walk through good grief as I release my pain and loss to You. Breath of God, breathe life into barren places. Lead me through good grief.
In Jesus' name, amen.

DAY 4

BIG LOSS

You shall love the LORD your God with all your heart, with all your soul, and with all your strength. And these words which I command you today shall be in your heart. You shall teach them diligently to your children and shall talk of them when you sit in your house, when you walk by the way, when you lie down, and when you rise up.

– Deuteronomy 6:5-7 NKJV

Have you suffered a big loss? No, I'm not referring to a sporting event or gambling loss but a life-altering loss: the loss of one of life's treasures. While loss is not insignificant, certain losses change us. My first BIG loss was my father. He shaped and molded my life. How? He corrected me with a stern look when I needed it. He showed me love every day. He taught me the value of grace and care for others. My father shared his love of God and God's Word. Since his death, I've shed countless tears and experienced deep, aching sadness, yet I'm also filled with fond memories and joyful moments of celebration. BIG loss affects my life every day. I am forever changed—changed and challenged to live and love.

Have you encountered BIG losses? Have you changed? Do you carry the legacy forward? Take a moment to reflect. Allow the legacy to live louder than the loss.

PRAY

Omnipotent God, nothing is too great for You. I am secure in Your divine power and authority. In Jesus' name, amen.

DAY 5

THIS IS FOR BELIEVERS

And now, dear brothers and sisters, we want you to know what will happen to the believers who have died so you will not grieve like people who have no hope. For since we believe that Jesus died and was raised to life again, we also believe that when Jesus returns, God will bring back with him the believers who have died.

– 1 Thessalonians 4:13-14 NLT

Why do we sometimes grieve like those without hope? Why do we wallow in grief and misery when our loved ones are rejoicing around Heaven? Would they want us to remain in misery and pain? When we are gone, is that the burden we want our loved ones to carry? Are we continuing their legacy or burying it in the depths of our despair? I asked and answered these questions in various seasons. I could not grieve without hope. I could not allow pain and misery to usurp the love and life given to me.

Have you allowed loss to rob you of joy? Joy in the life God has gifted to you? Joy in sharing life with others? Joy in spreading the Good News of Jesus to further the Kingdom of Heaven?

I want to LIVE despite loss because I am here for a reason. I believe God. Do you?

--- **PRAY** ---

Giver of life, I want to LIVE for YOU and share the light of those whose memory burns in my heart. In Jesus' name, amen.

DAY 6

BEYOND WHAT I SEE

So we don't look at the troubles we can see now; rather, we fix our gaze on things that cannot be seen. For the things we see now will soon be gone, but the things we cannot see will last forever.

– 2 Corinthians 4:18 NLT

Today, I am yielding, collapsing my will into His and relying on God's direction. I am tired, consumed with what I see rather than what God can and will do. A perfectly timed Bible study encouraged me to lean into the pastor's timely word delivered last evening. Think about this: what could our home, community, government, and world become if we transported our freedom—freedom not afforded to everyone around the world—and released it in worship beyond sanctuary walls and political platforms? What if we raised our hands to Heaven in praise while stopped at a traffic light or walking down the aisles of the grocery store praying for others? What if we helped the young family that looks different from us and expressed gratitude to the veteran proudly sporting his or her ball cap displaying service to our beloved nation? What if we paused to open our minds and hearts to receive the Holy Spirit?

If we all take this step, collapsing our will, we can realize what our home, community, government, and world can become.

I can see love moving in communities that help one another and share God. I can see a release of hatred and ignorance by talking, listening, and problem-solving amid differing opinions. I can see power and strength transforming lives rooted in the Holy Bible and led by the Holy Spirit.

Are you willing to see beyond?

PRAY

Patient God, teach me to yield and rely on You. Help me to see beyond my limited view. In Jesus' name, amen.

DAY 7

FORGIVE

I will give you a new heart and put a new spirit in you; I will remove from you your heart of stone and give you a heart of flesh. And I will put my Spirit in you and move you to follow my decrees and be careful to keep my laws. Then you will live in the land I gave your ancestors; you will be my people, and I will be your God.

– Ezekiel 36:26-28 NIV

How do you forgive? Do you have a heart of stone?

I do not know your journey and what experiences you have encountered, but I do know forgiveness is freeing. Forgiveness is for you to move forward, not for the one who wronged you. God wants you to release your transgressions, indiscretions, and purposeful wrongs toward others. Likewise, God wants you to release the transgressions and wrongs done to you. Matthew 6:14 says, "For if ye forgive men their trespasses, your heavenly Father will also forgive you" (KJV).

What area of your life needs forgiveness? Is your heart repentant? Has someone hurt you deeply, maybe unbearably? Your unforgiveness could be something petty that you refuse to release, perhaps a rivalry with someone from high school or college. It could be a grudge you are holding and cannot remember why. You have never shared the hurt because it is too painful to think about. It cuts too deeply into your core. How can you forgive? First, you must have the desire to forgive. Yes, whether you need to repent for wrongs you have done or release wrongs done to you, willingness to let go is before you.

Are you ready to let go of it? Really let go? Well, let go. It may take filling your mind one last time and speaking the shame, hurt, disappointment, bitterness, brutality, or hatred out of your life. Ask God to forgive you. He will. Ask God to help you forgive others; then forgive yourself. Forgive wrongdoers. Search your heart and release the pain.

PRAY

Heavenly Father, today, I am releasing _____. I am no longer trapped by unforgiveness. I am choosing to walk in freedom. I give the weight I have been carrying to you. You know the pain, despair, and root cause. Give me a clean heart and a fresh beginning. Thank You, God, that I can receive and grant forgiveness. In Jesus' name, amen.

DAY 8

PEACE

The God of peace will soon crush Satan under your feet. The grace of our Lord Jesus be with you.

– Romans 16:20 NIV

I awakened early and noticed Dr. David Jeremiah was preaching on the peace of God. Once again, the goodness of God overwhelmed me. His peace gives peace. When uncertainty and change surround me, God has settled my heart and quieted my spirit as I read Philippians 4:6-7: "Do not be anxious about anything, but in every situation, by prayer and petition, with thanksgiving, present your requests to God. And the peace of God, which transcends all understanding, will guard your hearts and minds in Christ Jesus" (NIV).

Am I the only one who allows anxiety and worry perpetuated by the enemy to unsettle me?
God, I am trusting in the shelter of Your wings (Psalm 61:1-4). There I find peace, the peace of God, God of peace within.

Moments ago, darkness filled the sky. The landscaping lights lifted a warm glow on the winter trees. Now, the sky brightens ever so slightly. I sit in anticipation of vibrant orange mingling with pale blue and creating beauty for all the Earth to see.

No matter where you are in life, remember darkness yields to light. Not sometimes, always. The absence of peace is dark, daunting, and scary. God's peace is light that does not diminish.

What darkness in your life can the peace of God shine in?

PRAY

God of peace, keep me in perfect peace. In Jesus' name, amen.

DAY 9

MY REFLECTION

So God created mankind in his own image, in the image of God he created them; male and female he created them.

– Genesis 1:27 NIV

Have you ever heard that you look like a parent or another relative—in essence, told you bear the image of someone else? How do you perceive and carry that image? Image bearer...those words stood out from my meeting notes. What kind of image bearer am I? Do I bear the image of the King of Kings, Lord of All? Of course, we have less than stellar moments called humanness. But, in totality, whose image is visible? Reflect on this verse: "As water reflects the face, so one's life reflects the heart" (Proverbs 27:19 NIV).

God sends reinforcements to incorporate into our lives when we earnestly seek and call on Him. I just received the book Holy Moments: A Handbook for the Rest of Your Life by Matthew Kelly, and shortly into the pages this quote rose from the page: "A still pond reflects the sun perfectly."

Recently, I enjoyed still moments when invited to attend a worship service with a dear friend. The presence of God filled the space as young and old sought after and praised God the Father, rejoiced in the resurrection of the Son, and manifested the movement of the Holy Spirit. It was powerful to witness unencumbered and uninhibited worship. The image of God was visible on the faces of men, women, and children.

Whose reflection do you see today? Do you like what you see? Take a quiet moment and be still. Reflect on the One whose image we are to bear and reflect. List ways you can become a better image bearer.

— **PRAY** —

Father, reveal Your reflection in me for others to see. In Jesus' name, amen.

DAY 10

SIGN SEEING

Ask the LORD your God for a sign, whether in the deepest depths or in the highest heights

– Isaiah 7:11 NIV

STOP!

We have all seen this octagon-shaped sign. Today it gave me cause to ponder. Traffic signs...do we obey them? Do we obey the signs and warnings we receive in other areas of our daily lives?

Are they as clear as road signs? Clear or not, I have disregarded road signs, both warning and cautionary. Likewise, I have seen other drivers ignore traffic signs. But why? The signs are there for our safety and protection. Why disregard them? We hurry from place to place, too busy to take precautions.

BUMP
TRAFFIC CALMING
NARROW ROAD
PROCEED WITH CAUTION

Do you have any signs laid out in front of you? STOP! Ask God for direction, and be obedient. Avoid the hazards and dangers of not exercising care.

— **PRAY** —

Heavenly Father, I want to see your signs and warnings. I want to be obedient and live in all You have for me. In Jesus' name, amen.

DAY 11

OUT ON A LIMB

For we live by faith, not by sight.

– 2 Corinthians 5:7 NIV

As I stood looking through a second-story picture window, I watched a squirrel move out on a limb. There was no hesitation, none. It was not concerned about the drop to the ground or whether the limb would sustain its weight. It focused on what it needed at the edge of the limb: food. Now that I think about it, I have never seen a squirrel fall from a tree. Have you? Squirrels do fall, but they scamper right back up. They climb, jump to adjacent branches, and move as freely off the ground as they do on the ground. I asked myself, "Why do I not have the same confidence? Why do I not step out on the limb freely, not concerned about the height or falling? Why does fear keep me hugging the tree?"

Do you have the confidence to step out on a limb? What you need may require you to move from comfortable footing and receive so much more. Whether you are in a comfortable position, desperate for change, or fearful, the time will come to step out on a limb. Are you willing to?
If I can do it, so can you. You are reading this book as a testament to what faith can do.
What made me think I could author a book? It is Who told me I could author a book: God. Sure, I love to write, but writing for enjoyment's sake and authoring a book are different undertakings. It took a while, but I was obedient. I had to trust God. I took a step in faith—faith to step out on a limb.

What do you need to trust God for and take a step in obedience?

PRAY

God, help me to always walk by faith and not by sight. In Jesus' name, amen.

DAY 12

DOES IT MATTER?

Though he slay me, yet will I trust in him: but I will maintain mine own ways before him.

– Job 13:15 KJV

Why bother doing what is right?

Have you ever asked that question? No matter what you do, something goes wrong. You are a good person, right? Life should go your way, right? Why are those doing wrong advancing? Does doing what is right—being kind, generous, faithful, compassionate, obedient, positive, forgiving, and gracious—matter?

The enemy is lurking, waiting for the moment to cause destruction. He wants you to doubt yourself. What can you do? Pray. Pray again. Read God's Word, the Holy Bible. Take the high road and hold no ill-will for others. Appreciate God's mercy and grace. Extend grace as you struggle to keep a cheery disposition. Don't allow the negative attempts to engage you in tug-o-war with these questions:

Why do others treat me poorly?
Why are agreements not kept?
Why do they want to crush my spirit?
Why? Why? Why?

Is there so much bitterness and lack of concern for others in our DNA? I do not believe that. Created beings exists to be in relationship with one another. Will we always agree? NO! Will we dislike the behavior of others (loved ones included)? Yes. However, we can still exhibit civility and humility. If you are unfamiliar with these principles, it is never too late to learn. Start with one action. Listen to someone with a varying opinion. Pray for someone who has been unpleasant and unkind. Shake off the bitterness and spewed venom hurled at you. Oh, I KNOW it is not easy. It takes grace and patience, but life will improve.

When your head is swirling and you feel defeated, trust God. Trust His Word and His actions. It matters.

PRAY

Heavenly Father, it matters. Help me to live in obedience and love because You are with me. In Jesus' name, amen.

DAY 13

MOVING ON

And my God will meet all your needs according to the riches of his glory in Christ Jesus.

– Philippians 4:19 NIV

The culmination of more than half my life's experience is approaching: the end of a marriage, my first marriage. I have experienced sadness and sorrow. I have experienced anger. I have experienced remorse. I have experienced pain. I have experienced joy. I have experienced love. And I have also triggered all these expressions. As the end draws closer, I reflect and ask God for mercy and lovingkindness. His goodness has been a shield and impenetrable protection. God's love has been present in the depths. When I could not feel Him close, He was there. God was there at heights when I could reach over and touch His powerful hand. God is here in the purging and packing. God is here as the last wanted items are loaded onto the truck. I wave and bid farewell to the past. The truck drives away. I am moving on and excited for a new beginning. I am relying on and trusting in my sovereign God.

For what do you need to rely on God? Do you trust that He will supply your needs?

--- **PRAY** ---

Sovereign God, Your goodness and mercy follow me. You have been faithful, and I trust You in new beginnings. In Jesus' name, amen.

DAY 14

FAREWELL AND HELLO

Therefore, if anyone is in Christ, the new creation has come. The old has gone, the new is here!

– 2 Corinthians 5:17 NIV

Farewell, past. You have drifted out to sea, never to return. And hello to what is to come on the horizon.

The past can be sharp and daunting. The past can hold the fondest memories and times of joy. But all of it—good, great, or weary to remember—is in the past. Grow and glean from it. Now it is time for farewell and to press forward into what today and tomorrow hold. So farewell, past, and hello to what is here and lies ahead.

--- **PRAY** ---

Father, thank You for farewells and hellos. Thank You for walking with me through whatever lies ahead. In Jesus' name, amen.

DAY 15

SEEDS AND SEASONS

They sowed fields and planted vineyards that yielded a fruitful harvest; he blessed them, and their numbers greatly increased, and he did not let their herds diminish.

– Psalm 107:37-38 NIV

How we long for a fresh relationship with You. Fresher than the first crisp, sweet bite of the autumn apple. Help us to delight in the season. Help us see and appreciate the changing temperatures. A new season is coming. The warmth of the sun begins to gradually lessen. The days become shorter. The extended periods of light are replaced by greater periods of darkness. I remind myself that the shortness of the day and the darkness is only for a season. Daylight always comes to chase the darkness. There's beauty in every season. Every season has a purpose (Ecclesiastes 3:1-8).

As coolness spans greater portions of the day, the leaves begin to turn and fall. Autumn arrives and brings with it the harvest. The yield is as bountiful as the planting; it reflects the sowing season (Galatians 6:7-9).

How bountiful is your harvest? What seeds have you sown? What kind of seeds? Are they seeds of faith to glorify God? Seeds of kindness to shine the light of Christ to all people? Seeds of love to cast out hatred? Seeds of truth to dispel the lies of the enemy? The lies, or should I say, believing the lies, interferes with our relationship with God. We cannot keep our relationship fresh when staleness—the enemy—creeps in through lies:

Why me? I am not capable.
Am I sure God wants me to do that?
Why should I help that person?
Why should I give a tithe/offering?
Why am I serving?

We do not always plant seeds that produce a harvest. Do you want a bountiful harvest? It is not too late—prepare yourself.

Autumn gives way to winter. It is a beautiful time when snow falls fresh over parts of the Earth. But it is cold, barren, and sometimes bitter. The harvest season has ended, and we are now preparing our soil for a period of dormancy. There we lie until it is time for the revival of life. Spring—a time of renewal. The sprouts of life come forth.

---- **PRAY** ----

God of Bounty, help us prepare for every season. We ask You to remove the desiccated, decayed leaves as we prepare for a new season. May the soil of our hearts be fertile and nurtured by Your Holy Spirit. Grow us to produce a bountiful harvest to share and glorify You. In Jesus' name, amen.

DAY 16

RAIN, RAIN, DO NOT GO AWAY

Ask the LORD for rain in the springtime; it is the LORD who sends the thunderstorms. He gives showers of rain to all people, and plants of the field to everyone.

– Zechariah 10:1 NIV

Rain serves so many purposes. We need rain to cool and replenish the Earth. It provides moisture for vegetation and plants. But our need for rain does not mean excitement follows. Today, rain and clouds cover everything I see. It is dreary. Yet, light is filtering my spirit. Soon the rain will give way to clear skies. I see light behind the clouds.

Some days, sunshine surrounds us, not a rain cloud in the sky. Eventually, rain comes. The skies in our lives darken. "Into each life some rain must fall," Henry Wadsworth Longfellow eloquently states in his work "Rainy Day." We need rainy days. Rain is refreshing and gloomy. I do not want the rain to go away and never return.

Ever notice the grass is taller and greener after the rain? The plants and flowers are lovelier. Yes, we need rain and clouds. Sunshine is not the same without it. I appreciate a sun-filled day after the dreariness dissipates. I need to remember that the next time I complain about the rain. God created the rain. God knows when to provide sun and rain over the Earth and in our lives. We need saturation. We are lifeless without it.

A realization just hit me. When my father passed away, a little piece of me died. Until this moment, I know I felt loss and every emotion of grief, but I buried a little bit of myself when the soil covered his casket. Now, that is not to say my soul is without sunshine or joy. You can experience loss, grief, despair, failure, hurt, and brokenness and still have joy. The sun's vast rays still extend. The God of hope is still ruler of all!

For everything there is a season (Ecclesiastes 3:1-8). You may be familiar with this passage of Scripture. Take a moment to read it. Because we have life, we have death. Death is not the end for those believing in the hope of

God. The dark skies and rain have a purpose and do not overshadow joy.

How has rain replenished you?

PRAY

Father, may rain replenish me as it replenishes the Earth. In Jesus' name, amen.

DAY 17

ROUND ABOUT

Show me the right path, O LORD; point out the road for me to follow. Lead me by your truth and teach me, for you are the God who saves me. All day long I put my hope in you.

– Psalm 25:4-5 NLT

My mother, the most beautiful, compassionate soul I know, has a great issue with roundabouts. I know she is not the only one. Is it difficult for you, too? I tell her to focus on the direction, not the roundabout. To stay in her lane but know whether the destination requires continuing straight or turning.

Are you entering a roundabout?

The direction and path that God has given us becomes more complicated when we focus on the turns of the roundabout rather than remaining in our lane and focusing on what God has for us. Knowing where we are going is important. But in life, we do not always know. So, just as in a roundabout, we yield before entering. We pray and seek God, collapsing our will into His. We receive a Word from God. The way becomes clearer, and we proceed with caution.

Notice that we yield before entering, but once inside, we must continue moving. So long as we remain in the proper lane, the roundabout will allow us to exit at the proper location. We must remain focused on where we are going—where God leads. Although circuitous, that roundabout is not as difficult to navigate when we yield (pray and collapse our will into His), enter with caution (receive a Word from the Lord) and exit properly (go where God leads).

Read Proverbs 4:25-27

PRAY

Omniscient God, help us to not overcomplicate life. Help us to rely on You and proceed in Your direction. In Jesus' name, amen.

DAY 18

GPS

He guides the humble in what is right and teaches them his way.

– Psalm 25:9 NIV

I do not remember a time when I doubted God's love for me. Sure, struggles and disappointments raised the "WHY?" question. But I know God loves me. Right now, I do not recall knowing and feeling the magnitude of God's love for me more than in this moment. It is overwhelming. Is anyone else feeling the same powerful, all-encompassing love? It's so indescribable, it hardly seems true. But it is true!

We allow distractions, often by the enemy, to derail us. What can we do? Focus on the love of God. Center on His Word. Fervently seek the presence of God. God really wants you to know and bask in His love, to know His desire for relationship with Him.

When I recede to a place of inner stillness, I can feel His presence. Now, I close my eyes and breathe in—breathe in fresh air to fill my spirit. I open my eyes to exhale, exhaling the staleness that tries to stagnate me. I am completely grateful to have a life filled with God's love and the love of others—love welcomed by the outpouring of His amazing grace. I am grateful for foundational love from parents who cherished one another, who built a home on a firm foundation of faith; for Christian love in a church community that heightens the meaning of agape love; for family love with those whom I share life's blood and the blood of Christ; for companion love from the man who holds my heart. Lord, I thank You.

Where this journey leads remains unknown, but it is going where God leads. How will I get there? God's guiding hand is the pathway. How will I connect with God? Those technologically aware (no, I am not one of you) know how to connect to a GPS (Global Positioning System). It provides the route. Follow the course, and you will not get lost. A GPS voice will even guide you. Hmmm, I have a voice that guides me, but I only hear it when

I listen. I remain on course when I follow the Map (Holy Scripture—the Word of God) and hear His voice. That voice is His whisper; it is the Holy Spirit, and it is hearing the Word from spiritual leaders. Will you allow the Holy Spirit and the Word of God to be your positioning system?

Read Proverbs 16:1-4

--- **PRAY** ---

Father, position me to align with You. May my heart be open and willing to abide in Your direction. In Jesus' name, amen.

DAY 19

LET FREEDOM RING

You, my brothers and sisters, were called to be free. But do not use your freedom to indulge the flesh; rather, serve one another humbly in love.

– Galatians 5:13 NIV

"I pledge allegiance to the flag of the United States of America, and to the Republic for which it stands, one Nation under God, indivisible, with liberty and justice for all."

I celebrate freedom woven into the fabric of our nation. I honor and cherish freedom of speech, freedom of religion, freedom of the press, freedom to peaceably assemble. We have freedom. And, as much as I love American freedom, the freedom granted by the death, life, and resurrection of Jesus is the greatest freedom—eternal freedom. Eternal freedom has no borders and is available to everyone (John 8:36, Galatians 5:1).

Speaking of freedom, I remember the Fourth of July after a trip abroad. It was a rainy, partly sunny day enjoyed in stages with family, friends, and the love of my life. As the day ended, I embraced the love of my life and silently prayed for safe travel on his mission trip the following day. As we departed, I looked up and there was a beautiful sign of God's promise...the rainbow. The storm had ended. God's faithfulness was beautifully and brilliantly arching the sky. I embraced freedom and expressed gratitude.

Proudly recite your expressions of freedom.

PRAY

Father, thank You for Your freedom. No matter where we are in the world, we have eternal liberty and life in You. In Jesus' name, amen.

DAY 20

EMOTIONAL OVERLOAD

From the end of the earth I will cry to You, When my heart is overwhelmed; Lead me to the rock that is higher than I. For You have been a shelter for me.

– Psalm 61:2-3 NKJV

Do you ever feel an emotional overload—frustration one minute and ready to burst into tears the next? You are not alone. Emotions run the gamut today while on my retreat. Melancholy, anger, and frustration each fight for a position. Anticipated snow accumulation has forced an adjustment of plans, extending the retreat. Do not misunderstand. I enjoy retreats—time away to reflect, to revel in the beauty of nature, and to see the splendor of glorious hues consuming the morning sky. But today, I just want to go home. Emotions fill me. I want comfort within the tranquility of my own surroundings. I want to come and go when the whim strikes. Walk to the pantry and raid the fridge for my favorite snacks. Bundle up in favorite blankets.

Hmmm, the petulant two-year-old emerges. I acknowledge it. I am sulking, pouting with tear-filled eyes. I am far too old to behave this way. How old is that? That is a conversation for another time. Time to draw in a deep breath and exhale the negative energy that has invaded my space. That helped. I draw in another deep breath to release the negative energy. As the evening sun settles across the sky, so do my emotions. Snow falls across the forest where deer are feeding. I smile as a single-antlered buck approaches a doe. A larger two-antlered buck appears and quickly chases the smaller buck away! Moments later, the single-antlered buck returns.

No matter what we face, nothing chases away God. Allowing God to intercede remedies emotional overload.

PRAY

Thank You, God for revealing beauty in every situation. Thank You for your calming presence. In Jesus' name, amen.

DAY 21

SIGN LANGUAGE

My sheep listen to my voice; I know them, and they follow me. I give them eternal life, and they shall never perish; no one will snatch them out of my hand.

– John 10:27-28 NIV

Who says we do not read building signs? I do. As a passenger during a short road trip, I noticed a church marquee sign that stated, "The closer we are to the Shepherd, the safer we are from the wolves." The attention-grabbing sign raised some questions: Am I close to the Shepherd? Am I safe from the wolves? How does being close to the Shepherd keep me safe?

Psalm 23:4 says, "Thy rod and Thy staff they comfort me" (KJV). If I am within reach of His rod and staff, I am close. I am safe.

Dependent sheep have protection and provision. They remain within the sound of the shepherd's voice. Do you trust the Shepherd? Are you within ear shot?

The book of Psalms is one of my favorites. David in his humble, earnest prayers, pleas, and songs trusted and relied on God. Have you memorized Psalm 23? Find a quiet place and read (or recite) the passage. Listen to the voice of the Shepherd.

PRAY

Father, keep us close to hear Your voice. Keep us close enough that Your rod and staff comfort, protect, and guide us. In Jesus' name, amen.

DAY 22

FLOAT ON

When the clouds are dark and heavy with rain, showers will fall upon the earth.

– Ecclesiastes 11:3 VOICE

As I drove across town, the weight of the clouds was lifting. My mind was full as the ominous sky was heavy with a cluster of dark clouds. It did not appear that the clouds were moving. They were. Both above and in my life. Suddenly, there was a beautiful sunset in view and the spectrum of a rainbow behind. The sky was brighter, and I felt lighter. The clouds were big, fluffy, effortlessly floating marshmallows.

Whatever you are facing, it will pass. But, in the moment, dark clouds loom. Life can be hard. Whatever you carry may seem unbearable. What are you carrying? What seems heaviest to bear? Psalm 55:22 says, "Cast your cares on the Lord and he will sustain you" (NIV).

Do not give up. Press in and float on.

--- **PRAY** ---

Lord, thank You for sustaining me. Whatever the day brings, Your love and grace allow me to press in and float on. In Jesus' name, amen.

DAY 23

PLEASE, NO DISTRACTIONS

Stay alert! Watch out for your great enemy, the devil. He prowls around like a roaring lion, looking for someone to devour.

— 1 Peter 5:8 NLT

It is winter in Florida. I am looking out the window mesmerized as the palm branches sway in unison while sunlight brightens their beautiful green hue. I hear their gentle rustle. My silent splendor is interrupted as landscapers begin their pruning. Although the noise of the equipment is a distraction, it does not negate the beauty before me. Their work enhances the beauty. I can choose to focus on the beauty in the sway of the palms or allow the noise to diminish its
beauty. Are you allowing distractions and interruptions to become your focus? Not me!

Do you have any noise or destruction interrupting the beauty surrounding you? What are you focused on today? Do you see beauty? Describe it.

Read Luke 10:38-42

PRAY

Faithful God, help me to focus on You and not allow distractions to interrupt Your beauty. In Jesus' name, amen.

DAY 24

RUFFLED FEATHERS

A hot-tempered person stirs up conflict, but one slow to anger calms strife

– Proverbs 15:18 CSB

There are days it is easy to ruffle my feathers. I awaken irritable, and the slightest action irks me. My inward focus is out of alignment.

Are your feathers ruffled, causing frustration or a short temper? No matter the cause, will you choose—yes, choose—to give praise? Do not allow anything to muffle your praise. Why? God inhabits the praises of His people (Psalm 22:3). Announce each day as the rooster does. Crow proudly and show the brilliant color God has given you. Your feathers will not ruffle so easily.

Lord, do not let my feathers get ruffled
So that my praise to You becomes muffled.

May my crow be proud and strong each day,
Receiving Your grace in a fresh, new way.

Such beautiful colors You have placed on me,
A brilliant spectrum for all to see.

PRAY

Lord, reduce my ruffles and increase my praise. In Jesus' name, amen.

DAY 25

SWEET SOUND

The birds of the sky nest by the waters; they sing among the branches.

– Psalm 104:12 NIV

Once again, the beauty of nature captivates my attention and immerses me in its call. I sit outside and inhale the fresh fragrance as my eyes move from tree to tree with the birds. I join them in harmonious worship.

I hear the sweet sound of the birds in my ear,
Their tunes are joyful, pleasant, and clear.

I cannot help but wonder how pleased God must be,
To hear his creation express so exuberantly.

The gift of nature a treasure for sure,
It is beautiful, boundless, and pure.

Let us lift our eyes together in praise,
All His creations, be forever amazed.

Find a space to sit, worship, and sing before the Lord. Your vocal abilities are not important. Your sincere heart to worship will be a sweet sound rising to Heaven. Enter His presence reciting this psalm: "Worship the LORD with gladness; come before him with joyful songs" (Psalm 100:2 NIV).

PRAY

Father, thank You for the sweet sounds You have created. Thank You for the wonderful and boundless beauty that surround us. Open our ears and eyes to enjoy all You have made for us as expressions of Your enduring love. In Jesus' name, amen.

DAY 26

WARM FUZZIES

You keep him in perfect peace whose mind is stayed on you, because he trusts in you.

– Isaiah 26:3 ESV

What thoughts fill your head? I have days when my mind bounces from thought to thought, never holding one for long. Other days, negative thoughts attack my mind. That is when the Word of God becomes a weapon. Proverbs 4:23 says, "Carefully guard your thoughts because they are the source of true life" (CEV). Or, as another translation says, "Protect your mind, for life flows from it"(CEB).

Memorize a verse that you can recite anytime. When you do not have a verse, reach for the Word of God, the Holy Bible. If your thoughts are affirming, hold and expand them. If they are negative and depleting, replace them... immediately.

This poem below is titled "Warm Fuzzies." My thoughts were occupied with remembering love's journey.

Thoughts of you fill my head,
I still remember the first thing you said.

Incredible to believe this journey's begun,
A love story created by omniscient One.

You and I could not fabricate this dream,
Woven into a well-knotted seam.

Let us embrace this love that springs forth,
It points straight to our True North.

PRAY

Father, life is not always "warm fuzzies," but help us to focus our thoughts on the love we give, the love we receive, and the promises Your Word delivers. In Jesus' name, amen.

DAY 27

BOUND AS ONE

Be devoted to one another in love. Honor one another above yourselves.

– Romans 12:10 NIV

I learned from my parents that marriage is sacred. They honored their commitment to one another and God. Their love and devotion permeated every area of life, including mine. The vow of marriage is more than a ritual. It is a covenant of three—a commitment between you, your spouse, and God. Marriage is a binding of life together. I missed the mark the first time. Thankfully, grace has given me another chance. I share my wisdom in this poetic reflection written for my son's wedding.

Bound As One

May your wedding day overflow with tears of joy and laughter,
Bound as one always thereafter.

Center your love with God in between,
In every circumstance, on Him to lean.

Life narrows and widens, that is for sure,
Road mapped together, your love will endure.

From this day forward, bid farewell to the past,
Goodness and peace to cherish at last.

So, here is to you and the love you share,
A candle glowing here, there, and everywhere.

You are loved by God and me,
Forever, for always, it will be.

Whether married or not, bonds with others are adhesive. We are one body in Christ. What bonds do you share? Build connection and meaningful relationships. There are none more important than our relationship with God. Create a bond with Him and others. Love one another (John 13:34).

— **PRAY** —

Loving God, bind us together in Your love and unity. In Jesus' name, amen.

DAY 28

PROVISION

The LORD will guide you always; he will satisfy your needs in a sun-scorched land and will strengthen your frame. You will be like a well-watered garden, like a spring whose waters never fail.

— Isaiah 58:11 NIV

Are you involved in your church or local community? Are you sharing what God has given you?

I was serving in our children's ministry, and the group leaders asked the class to share what the story was about. The lesson was teaching the story of the widow God told Elijah to seek out (1 Kings 17:7-16). We learned that the land was without rain and God told Elijah to go to Zarephath. He obeyed. There, he encountered and called out to the widow, asking for water and bread. The widow replied that she had barely enough flour and oil for her last meal with her son. You see, the widow and her son were planning to die because of lack. But wait...Elijah told the widow to prepare what she had. First, she was to bring a small portion to him and then prepare a meal for herself and her son. By doing so, she would not be without (lack) flour or oil until God replenished their land with rain. The widow obeyed. She decided to trust God to satisfy her needs. Do you?

Twice in the story the class learned about obedience. One student pointed out that we do not always listen to God. It is true; we do not. This lesson reminds us God is true to His Word. The widow did not lack the food she needed. This story has me pondering these questions:

Am I preparing for death, lacking what I need?
Do I feel less valuable in tough times?
Do I have unwavering faith that God will meet my needs?

It is difficult to intentionally share when you barely have enough to survive. Imagine the widow's concern. How would she provide for herself and her son? What a challenge to give when you are uncertain of your next provision! Obedience and reliance on God are game changers. Be willing to listen and obey, even if it requires you to serve others.

PRAY

Gracious God, help us to be obedient to You whether we are coming out of barrenness, seeking water and bread, or called to share what we have in faith, knowing You provide. We will never lack what we need when trusting and relying on You. We give You all the glory in our blessing and abundance. In Jesus' name, amen.

DAY 29

CHRISTMAS LOOK UP

And God is able to make all grace overflow to you, so that, always having all sufficiency in everything, you may have an abundance for every good deed.

– 2 Corinthians 9:8 NASB

I love Christmas. I love hearing the Christmas story read during Christmas Eve service and imagining Jesus lying in a manger with the Star of Bethlehem above, guiding the Wise Men. I love preparing meals, wrapping presents, and decorating the tree topped with a star. I love sharing everything that is Christmas.

Christmas preparations are almost complete; one last package to send. This morning, I was determined to wrap and box the items and head out to ship the box. There was one slight problem: I forgot about a box. I scurried about looking for a packing solution. It was a Goldilocks moment. The bubble packaging envelopes were too small, and the box in plain view was too large. I checked closets for a box while fully expecting a drive to the store before completing the package shipping task. As I opened the hall closet and looked up, there was a box. It looked like the perfect size. Could it be? I took down the box, which held votives, and packed the Christmas gift items. The box was just the right size. If I had not taken a moment to search, I would not have found what I needed. It was there the whole time.

Sometimes, we just need to search and then look up. Reflect on a moment when grace was sufficient.

PRAY

Father, thank You for providing all we need. Thank You for Your voice that guides, directs, and encourages us to look up. Your door is open and grace overflows. In Jesus' name, amen.

DAY 30

SEEING WONDER

On the glorious splendor of your majesty, and on your wondrous works, I will meditate.

– Psalm 145:5 ESV

Sightseeing is one of the pleasures of traveling. Vistas are never the same. Noticing the clouds meeting the mountains is breathtaking. The mist and river gorges below are astounding.

Do you take in the scenery when you travel? You may not have an impressive mountain view, but see astonishment in your surroundings. Carry that view throughout the day. I have discovered that beauty is all around us. No matter the frustrations, the fears, the anxieties, or the headaches, something beautiful is close by (1 Chronicles 29:11).

Take a moment from your busyness and see wonder. Jot down what you see.

PRAY

Magnificent God, help me to see Your splendor every day. May I be astonished and thankful for each view. In Jesus' name, amen.

DAY 31

DECEMBER SKY

The heavens declare the glory of God; the skies proclaim the work of his hands.

– Psalm 19:1 NIV

It is a vast, pleasant December sky. The hues are marvelous blues. The birds are talking to one another in splendid harmony. The squirrels are scampering down the bird houses, having absconded with bird feed. The air is crisp and unseasonably calm. I watch and listen in awe. The vibrant colors, the sounds, the splendor all quiets me to tranquility.

Have you noticed the sky today? Are there rain clouds, gray skies, or sunshine?

PRAY

God of all seasons, thank You for nature and its splendid harmony. In Jesus' name, amen.

DAY 32

THE FLOWERS FADE

The grass withers, the flower fades, but the word of our God will stand forever.

– Isaiah 40:8 ESV

My husband and I were experimenting in flower preservation. As part of my birthday celebration, we went to see Wayne Newton: Up Close and Personal. We were sitting front and center. At the end of the show, Wayne gathered two beautiful red rose corsages. The first rose was given to an older woman also on the front row. The other rose—you guessed it...yes! Wayne walked toward me. I was excited. It was my second encounter in two years. The first was a photo op in Las Vegas.

Well, back to flower preservation. My husband and I obtained the molds and epoxy mixture to prepare the rose. Well, the rose shriveled in the mixture. My mind thought of Isaiah 40:8. Fortunately, I had removed petals and laminated them. The memory was preserved in my mind. The corsage, well, it was a "work of art." That is what we are calling it—"a work of art"!

The Word of God is a work of art that will never fade.

PRAY

Masterful God, preserve me forever. In Jesus' name, amen.

DAY 33

WAITING...

Wait on the LORD; Be of good courage, and He shall strengthen your heart; Wait, I say, on the LORD!

– Psalm 27:14 NKJV

"Are we there yet?" Do you remember asking that question on a long (or short) road trip? You wanted to reach the destination. As a child, I recall looking out the window to count different states' license plates. It helped the time pass.

Are you waiting? Are you waiting patiently?

I have more than one answer to that question. It depends on the waiting time and what the wait is for. Is the wait for a busy server to bring meals while the aromas of food surround? Is the wait for confirmation of good news?

So, how do you behave while waiting? Again, it depends on the waiting time, but should it? The phrase "patience is a virtue" comes to mind. I must say, I have work to do because "I want it now!" rears up. Am I the only one?

We have hurried and busy lives. Drivers cut us off while changing lanes. Vehicles speed down the highway like race cars. Gadgets occupy our hands while waiting. Home life can be a revolving door, dashing to activities. You get the idea.

What if God were as impatient with us? He is patient, and we should try harder to be (2 Peter 3:9). Why be patient? As the proverb goes, "Good things come to those who wait." More importantly, God's timing is… PERFECT!

List ways you can practice patience.

PRAY

Lord, help us to see You in the busyness and slow down! In Jesus' name, amen.

DAY 34

BEDTIME BONNET

Share each other's burdens, and in this way obey the law of Christ.

– Galatians 6:2 NLT

It was time for bed. Time for the hair bonnet that I remembered to grab from the drawer and place on the nightstand. I had just finished praying with my hands touching the wood and metal cross hanging on the wall. It is not only symbolic but sentimental. The cross was a gift from my husband while he was away serving on a mission trip. I walked back into our bedroom and looked at the nightstand—no bonnet. I looked around. Did it fall? No bonnet. My husband asked what I was looking for. He knew. I brushed him off (lovingly, of course). He asked again as I left the room. Finally, I replied, "I'm looking for my bonnet." His reply: "I thought so. It's on your head!"

Anyone else have a little stubbornness? All I needed to do was ask for help, state my need, to find what I was looking for. Instead, I walked around looking for what was right there.

When you need help, ask.

--- **PRAY** ---

Lord, I need help. You have placed others in my life for support. Help me to put aside pride and ask. In Jesus' name, amen.

DAY 35

GIVING THANKS

Oh, give thanks to the LORD, for He is good! For His mercy endures forever.

– 1 Chronicles 16:34 NKJV

I messaged back and forth with a friend regarding Thanksgiving meal plans, wondering if she and her new beau would be sharing part of the day together. A childish grin covered my face, and butterflies filled my abdomen as I remembered my first major holiday celebration with my husband before we were married. It was a Thanksgiving to remember. Gratitude and excitement filled my cornucopia to overflowing in abundance, a "horn of plenty."

As I inhale and exhale, I thank You, God,
Life still flows in this old bod.

Giving thanks in more ways than I can count,
Blessings overflow from a Heavenly fount.

This Thanksgiving is here for limited hours.
But my gratitude carries forth daily power.

Take a moment to express gratitude. Gratitude for every blessing.

Jeremiah 30:19 (ESV): "Out of them shall come songs of thanksgiving, and the voices of those who celebrate."
1 Chronicles 29:13 (ESV): "And now we thank you, our God, and praise your glorious name."

PRAY

Merciful God, thank You for life, love, friendship, and your abundance of goodness. My heart overflows. In Jesus' name, amen.

DAY 36

REFLECTIONS

Those who are right with God are remembered with honor, but the name of the sinful will waste away.

– Proverbs 10:7 NLV

Memories and emotions flood my mind as the day draws to a close. My late father's birthday approaches, which triggers pangs of grief and fond memories. All who have experienced significant loss can relate. Reflecting reminds me to treasure the moments past and to capture new ones.

My father taught me to drive. At the time, I was not a fan of parallel parking. Well, guess what we spent more time on than anything? That is right, parallel parking! I am so glad we did. Not only did I ace that section of the exam but every other part, too. (Feel free to chuckle here.) I thank my dad when backing up or parallel parking. It is a small memory, but I carry it with me.

What small memories do you carry? Does it warm your heart to remember?

PRAY

Father, we have varied reflections. May we hold dear cherished memories and remember the love and kindness shown to us. In all we do, keep us mindful of Your enduring love for us. In Jesus' name, amen.

DAY 37

DREAMS DO COME TRUE

It is pleasant to see dreams come true, but fools refuse to turn from evil to attain them. Walk with the wise and become wise; associate with fools and get in trouble.

– Proverbs 13:19-20 NLT

Have you ever forgotten what it is like to dream? Forgotten what it is like to float and experience joy in the moment? Rather, you feel caught in the minutia of life and just go through the motions, not fully living life...merely existing.

We should dream. Dream and strive to make our dreams reality. Psalm 37:4 reminds us that God will give us the desires of our hearts. He wants us to have joy. But we have work to do.

What are your dreams? What does your heart desire? Are you willing to seek God and His plan, to realize what is in your heart, what God planted within you?

I can tell you I had stopped dreaming. I just began existing, and every area of my life was a reflection. Sure, the brave face was on, but inwardly, there was barrenness. I masked it. I am not certain I realized how deep the chasm was. Over time, I really sought to find where God was leading me. I was wandering. There were no goals for me, personally. Sure, I accomplished tasks for my various commitments, but not for me. This lasted more than a year and a half. It took a bit, and I am not there yet. Notice I said yet? The Spirit of God is moving.

A couple of years ago, I went to Israel. Life changes were in motion. God moved. I was faithful to His prompting. The journey to Israel changed the trajectory of my life. I encountered God's love as never before and experienced a glimpse of the life of my Lord and Savior, Jesus Christ. Each day of the trip, it was as if a little more of me was returning to life. I still had no solid direction, but I knew God wanted more of me and more for my life. One specific memory was prayer in the Garden of Gethsemane where Jesus was face down, requesting of His Father to let the cup pass from Him (Matthew 26:39). I could feel the gravity of the space. I touched a 2,500-year-old tree and absorbed how that incredible mass of wood existed when Jesus called to Heaven. As I waited to pray with my pastor, I walked the garden from end to end, praying, crying, and thanking Jesus for His sacrifice to save me. Thanking a God who could love us so much that He gave His only begotten Son to free us from our sin. You know the verse—John 3:16.

I fervently prayed to change my life. Intentionally, I released brokenness and failure and claimed a new life. I prayed prayers of repentance for my failed marriage and relationships, prayers for healing and a right relationship with a God who knows my heart, prayers for love and life in the will of God. Heaven was listening. The plates were shifting.

Speak your dreams. Heaven is listening.

PRAY

Heavenly Father, I place my dreams in Your hands. In Jesus' name, amen.

DAY 38

ARMORED PRAYER

Put on the full armor of God, so that you can take your stand against the devil's schemes.

– Ephesians 6:11 NIV

Do you pray for your mate, partner, spouse or loved one?

I pray for others, but for no one more than my husband. It is necessary to cover those we love continually in prayer. Prayers for protection, provision, guidance, wisdom, health, discipleship, discernment, and care. I want to see God at work in and through my husband, our marriage, and our lives—all of which require prayer. Prayer is a daily and nightly ritual for gratitude, guidance and, in this instance, armor.

I awakened early with this prayer in my heart for my husband from head to toe. As you pray this prayer, incorporate your loved ones.

A prayer for my husband:

Father, I pray the blessing of Heaven begins with his head, Lord. May he always see, read, hear, and comprehend Your Word. Cover him with the helmet of salvation. Grant him extraordinary wisdom and insight into business and our finances. Let his voice sing and shout Your praise all day long. Bless his eyesight to see clearly and receive Your view of things. Bless his arms with strength to lift others and to envelop me, his wife. May he carry the Sword of the Spirit to support and defend the faith. Bless everything he touches. Bless his heart with Your love for all people and fill him with Your Holy Spirit every day of his life. Protect him with the breastplate of righteousness and shield of faith. May Your love overflow in him and grow deeper. Gird his loins with truth to withstand the enemy's lies, attacks, and deceptions. Keep his legs strong and healthy to walk in faith. Shod his feet with the preparation of the gospel of peace, bound to share the Good News of the Kingdom of God. Help him walk firmly in Your way, Lord.

Read Ephesians 6:10-18 and strategically pray for others.

— **PRAY** —

God, may Your glory shine through my husband's life. In Jesus' name, amen.

DAY 39

MOURNING HOPE

I will turn their mourning into joy. I will comfort them and exchange their sorrow for rejoicing.

– Jeremiah 31:13 NLT

Mourning is the intimate, personal part of loss. We can suppress it, run from it. Eventually, it catches us. Patiently, sorrow will wait until acknowledged. It may be delayed, but it remains. It does not seem real. But IT IS REAL. It leaves us grappling to balance loss and yet move forward.

A close friend asked if I was angry over loss in my life. My answer was and is no. Love permeates my life, and that love is reciprocal. Necessary lessons have been taught. Reliance on God and His faithfulness in all circumstances has been put to the test. How I wish the outcomes were different, that my loved ones' good health was not accosted, but I TRUST God. Everything I have learned and believe in is before me, on display for all to see.

What is my witness? Yes, I am in mourning. Yes, I have deep sorrow. Yes, loss is painful. However, this is not the end of the story. I have HOPE. HOPE in the foundation of God that penetrated my soul at the age of four. HOPE in the God who WAS, IS, and ALWAYS will be. HOPE in the continual love, prayer and compassion of others who bless my life immeasurably. Psalm 30:5 is a reminder that sorrow is temporary: "Weeping may endure for a night; but joy comes in the morning (NKJV)."

List your sorrow and your hope. Write down a scripture to recite over your sorrow.

PRAY

God of Hope, You are faithful. I trust You. In Jesus' name, amen.

DAY 40

THE SEARCH IS OVER

If you look for me wholeheartedly, you will find me.

– Jeremiah 29:13 NLT

Have you found everything you are looking for in life? The career you always wanted with the nest egg for retirement. The love of family and friends you gather and share life with. The perfect, well-appointed home to enjoy. The life of traveling to faraway places. Or are you searching for anything? Searching for love, friendship, companionship, answers, connection, happiness, peace, tranquility, or the fulfillment of your purpose. You are not alone. I am a child, looking for God. We are all searching—searching for Him everywhere. He is all around.

Where are you searching? Seek God in prayer. Open His Word, the Holy Bible, and search no more. God is all around, lifting the veil of His power. Power in the tree rooted by waters and its sway in the breeze. Power in the sunshine. Power in the movement of the clouds. Power in the birds that glide and soar. Power in the crash of the waves. Power in the still of the night sky lit by the moon and bright stars. Power to move in your life.

What are you looking for? Where will you go to find it? God is within you. God is within me. The search is over.

―――― **PRAY** ――――

God, I have sought and found You. I search no more. Thank You for rescuing me. In Jesus' name, amen.

DAY 41

BLESSED ASSURANCE

Let us draw near to God with a sincere heart and with the full assurance that faith brings, having our hearts sprinkled to cleanse us from a guilty conscience and having our bodies washed with pure water.

– Hebrews 10:22 NIV

Awakened by early light, I hear Fanny Crosby's "Blessed Assurance" playing in my head. My subconscious knew I needed reassurance. I know I should not worry but cast my cares on God (1 Peter 5:7). I fall short; I do worry about the unknown. Life's challenges require me to draw on strength far exceeding my own. I move on in faith as a new chapter continues to unfold. Faith that God's Word is true. Faith that the enemy's presence is no match for God. Nothing can separate me from His love. I will stand confident in God's assurance, confident as an heir of salvation because of the blood of Jesus.

Although I have confidence and credence as I move forward, fear still shows up. What fears do you need God's assurance spoken over? Name them. Songs of affirmation and the Word of God sealed within us provide security.

What songs do you hear? Are they songs of affirmation? Jot them down.

Read Romans 8:31-39 aloud.

God is with you. God is for you. Blessed assurance! "This is my story; this is my song: praising my Savior all the day long."

PRAY

Loving God, thank You for the songs of faith I hear. Thank You for the assurance you provide. In Jesus' name, amen.

DAY 42

KNOWING HIS VOICE

My sheep listen to my voice; I know them, and they follow me.

– John 10:27 NIV

A dear friend and spiritual mentor reminded me that the answers to our questions are in God's Word. Seek Him and find Him (Isaiah 55:6). Seek God. He will reveal Himself. He wants a relationship. He wants closeness and intimacy with us. He already knows our hearts. He knows our despair. He knows our desires (pure and unpure). He knows our deficiencies and capabilities. We find strength and sufficiency as we draw near Him.

James 4:8 is a reminder that when you draw near to God, He will draw near to you. If you are quiet and still in this moment, do you feel His presence? Beginning this introspection has allowed me to weep—lament—see areas of needed growth, see God's love, acknowledge sin and my deficiency, ask for and receive forgiveness, and enter His presence. Remember, God is a safe haven—the ULTIMATE haven—and He will take what was meant for your harm and turn it for good! (Genesis 50:20). Are you realizing and experiencing the power of God's love for you? The power of God's Word? It breathes life into us.

Psalm 23 is one of my favorite passages of Scripture. I learned to recite it as a child, but I did not understand the depths of David's song until later in life. Read and absorb the psalm: "The LORD is my shepherd; I shall not want" (KJV). He knows us as a shepherd knows his sheep. And His sheep know Him. They know the sound of the Shepherd's voice.

I have a friend who is a shepherd. I was amazed that when he calls his sheep, they respond to his voice without hesitation. They know and respond to the call of their shepherd. David was a
shepherd and understood the Lord as his shepherd. So, he did not want. He knew the Shepherd would provide and care for him. David trusted God. The LORD is my shepherd; I shall not want. Everything we need, the Lord provides.

Read Psalm 23.

PRAY

Lord, my Shepherd, I want to hear You and know Your voice. In Jesus' name, amen.

DAY 43

HE CALLS MY NAME

But now says the LORD, he who created you O Jacob, he who formed you, O Israel: "Fear not, for I have redeemed you; I have called you by name, you are mine.

– Isaiah 43:1-2 ESV

My husband and I were traveling. I had just finished a cup of tea when he called my name. His low, deep voice was gentle and kind. He was outside and wanted me to see an animal he had never seen before. By the time I had placed my cup and saucer down, the animal was gone. Returning to sit and gaze at the ocean, I pondered whether we hear God call our name. Do we have that intimate, loving relationship with Him? I do not believe we can ever become too close to God. I long to hear Him call my name and know, unequivocally, that God is calling me. Just like I had no doubt my husband was calling my name.

Do you hear God calling your name? How will you respond?

PRAY

Loving God, I want to be close to You. I want to hear Your voice. In Jesus' name, amen.

DAY 44

SPEAK THE NAME OF JESUS

And whatever you do, whether in word or deed, do it all in the name of the Lord Jesus, giving thanks to God the Father through him.

– Colossians 3:17 NIV

When I have difficulty sleeping, I pray. Sometimes I turn on the television, but my initial reaction is to begin a conversation with God. I thank Him for the things we often take for granted, like fresh air in our lungs and the ability to move, think, and speak. I talk to God as a confidante and friend. I listen, too. I pray for others. I speak the name of Jesus over individuals, entities, and circumstances. Jesus. Do you realize the power in His name? Think for a moment how amazing it is to speak a name that carries all power, authority, healing, and comfort. The name is Jesus.

I not only speak the name of Jesus, but others speak His divine name on my behalf. If your phone or device is handy, send the name JESUS to someone—just type JESUS.

Go a step further and verbally speak His name over situations, relationships, loved ones, those needing love, or whatever comes to mind.

I speak the name of Jesus over you. JESUS.

PRAY

Father, thank You for Your Son, Jesus. His name is power. In Jesus' name, amen.

DAY 45

GLIMMER OF HOPE

My hope comes from him. Truly he is my rock and my salvation.

– Psalm 62:5-6 NIV

Oftentimes, words capture what you feel. But there are moments when words feel pressed down by the weight of brokenness and despair. Crushing weight destroys confidence and seeks to pulverize hope. You do not feel strong. You do not feel empowered. You do not feel capable. You do not feel valuable.

Do not give up. You do have a glimmer of hope. You do have a mustard seed of faith. Is it enough? In Matthew 17:20-21 (NIV), Jesus replied, "Because you have so little faith. Truly I tell you, if you have faith as small as a mustard seed, you can say to this mountain, 'Move from here to there,' and it will move. Nothing will be impossible for you.'" So, is a glimmer of hope, a mustard seed of faith, enough? Yes, yes, it is!

The smallest amount of light penetrates the darkness. Recently, I looked at a closed blind. Through the slats, the brilliance of the streetlight still pierced the slightest opening. That is hope: it gives light. That is God: He gave us Light.

Read these passages of Scripture to encourage you in hope:

Romans 15:13: "May the God of hope fill you with all joy and peace as you trust in Him, so that you may overflow with hope by the power of the Holy Spirit" (NIV).

Psalm 71:14: "As for me, I will always have hope. I will praise you more and more" (NIV).

Joshua 1:9: "Be strong and of good courage" (NKJV).

When my father passed, the hymn "All My Hope Is in Jesus" played continuously in my head. The Sunday before his death, our church praise band sang that song; it was a hauntingly beautiful reminder of all we have in Jesus.

All my hope is in Jesus, my Living Hope. May the God of hope fill you.

PRAY

Father, You are hope in brokenness and despair. I will praise you in all that I go through. In Jesus' name, amen.

DAY 46

PUT YOUR HANDS TOGETHER

In his hand is the life of every creature and the breath of all mankind.

– Job 12:10 NIV

Have you ever thought about how hands interlock? Probably not. This morning, I was thinking about the connection felt when hands clasp together, when your fingers intertwine with the one you love. Then I clasped my hands together. Albeit amazing and heartwarming when we clasp our hands, it is God's hand that cradles all things (Colossians 1:17).

My and my beloved's hands in union still pales in comparison with my fingers collapsing together in prayer to God. Have you noticed that? Try it. Is it a coincidence? My answer is no. Our left and right hands connect perfectly by design. Hands that join with another's during a walk or when showing support and love connect to fold in prayer to God, the Father. Everything under Heaven has a purpose. That includes you, me, and our hands.

Clasp your hands together. Close your eyes and be in unison with God. Welcome His love.

--- **PRAY** ---

God of creation, thank You for Your connection, love, and purpose so perfectly designed. In Jesus' name, amen.

DAY 47

FLYING HIGH

Who are these that fly along like clouds, like doves to their nests?

– Isaiah 60:8 NIV

As you can tell by now, poetry is a way of expression for me. Every season of my life remains marked by poetry. "Flying High" (below) depicts God's faithfulness in answered prayer. God was faithful in the valley. As mentioned before, I do not like waiting patiently. However, I am learning to do so. Why? Things take time. Everything does not occur in my timing. Nothing occurs in my timing. It is God's timing (Psalm 27:14). It can be a difficult lesson to learn, but relying on God's timing will allow you to soar higher.

Nestled so close, your voice in my ear,
That smooth, deep voice is clear.

You utter softly of what is to be,
While holding me oh, so lovingly.

My heartbeat and yours, combined into one,
The cord of three, woven and spun.

God, our Father, remain in between,
This poetically beautiful, loving scene.

We waited and prayed, for timing exactly right,
My heart was like a kite, lifted in flight.

Do not ever doubt my love for you,
It burns bright, through and through.

How do you express yourself? Journal or reflect on a lighthearted moment.

PRAY

Heavenly Father, we can fly high because You are with us. Your love is with us. And Your timing is exactly right. In Jesus' name, amen.

DAY 48

NEW DAY DAWNING

The night is far spent, and the day is at hand: let us therefore cast off the works of darkness, and let us put on the armor of light.

– Romans 13:12 ASV

Day is breaking. I cannot see the sun, but glimmers of light are visible, reflective of how I feel. One lone plane is descending in preparation for landing. The sky is silent, no birds in motion or chirping. Last night's slumber did not release yesterday's dreariness. I have a choice: Embrace the newness of today or remain in yesterday.

How are you feeling today? Are you a ray of sunshine or a rain cloud waiting to downpour on those around you?

Today you can be the appearance of light and begin anew. I plan to. It is a new day:
"A new day will dawn for us from above because our God is loving and merciful. He will give light to those who live in the dark and in death's shadow" (Luke 1:78-79 GW).

Will you embrace the light of the new day?

--- **PRAY** ---

God of the new day, thank You for light and mercy, new every morning. You cast off the darkness. In Jesus' name, amen.

DAY 49

MOONLIGHT GAZE

Once for all, I have sworn by my holiness—and I will not lie to David—that his line will continue forever and his throne endure before me like the sun; it will be established forever like the moon, the faithful witness in the sky.

– Psalm 89:35-37 NIV

Does loneliness smother you when a loved one is away, or do you look forward to time apart? I count down the moments until my loved one and I are together again. At nightfall, I gaze at the moon we share and feel a connection. Are you far from a loved one, far apart in distance or far apart in connection? How will you connect with them to feel close? If you are far apart in connection, your call or message may receive no response. However, there is a connection with no rejection. Connecting with Him may also reconnect disconnection with others. God, the Creator of the bright night moon, wants a close connection with you. His love and mercy endure (Psalm 136:9).

The Moon

The light of the moon, hung in the sky,
Place there for us to look up high.

Full of beauty, for both to see,
It lessens the separation 'tween you and me.

So, gaze at the moon above,
I will look too and send my love.

Someday soon, the distance will part,
Oh, how you fill my heart.

PRAY

*Father, thank You for heavenly light that connects us to one another and You.
In Jesus' name, amen.*

DAY 50

WHAT REMAINS

The Mighty One, God, the LORD, speaks and summons the earth from the rising of the sun to where it sets.

– Psalm 50:1 NIV

It is a beautiful sunset. The waves crash and roll. The breeze is cooler now, and the sun's warmth is fleeting. Footprints of activity cover the sand. I capture a mental image to hold this single moment. The setting sun will rise again tomorrow. The clouds will move; new ones will appear. The mortal footprints in the sand will wash away with the tide. The sky will remain. I praise God for what remains.

The next time you see a sunset, praise the name of the Lord.

"From the rising of the sun to its going down, The LORD's name is to be praised" (Psalm 113:3 NKJV).

PRAY

Heavenly Father, thank You for Your eternal presence. In Jesus' name, amen.

DAY 51

THREE RS

Therefore, we do not lose heart. Though outwardly we are wasting away, yet inwardly we are being renewed day by day.

– 2 Corinthians 4:16 NIV

Redeemed. Restored. Renewed.

I am going to date myself here. Growing up, the three Rs of learning were Reading, Writing, and Arithmetic. Reading and writing have always been my favorites. Grasping these fundamental building blocks still has merit. However, the three Rs described today represent redeemed, restored, and renewed.

Redemption is ours through the blood of Jesus, who sacrificed His life to save all of us. Christ paid for our sins so that salvation would be available to us. There will never be a greater sacrifice. Tell yourself, "Jesus redeemed me." Do you believe it? God's Word says:
"In him we have redemption through his blood, the forgiveness of our trespasses, according to the riches of his grace" (Ephesians 1:7 NASB).

Redemption is yours because of Jesus' sacrifice to save us.

Our redemption allows for our restoration. We enter into our right place in relationship with God. We repent from our wrongdoings and desire to live for God; we trust and honor Him more than anything else. Restoration is yours! Ask God to restore you no matter what has happened in the past.

Restoration requires a little work because we sin. We stray from the right path. We choose to go our own way instead of following God's path. Are you doing the work to be in relationship with God? If not, start today and begin an eternal relationship (Psalm 23:3). Read David's Psalm 51:12 cry, "Restore to me the joy of Your salvation, and uphold me with a willing spirit" (ESV).

Are you crying out to God?

Because of redemption and restoration, we can experience renewal.

Renewal is a continuation of restoration. We can resume where we stray from the right path. It is exciting to know that these three Rs are building blocks for our eternal lives. Psalm 51:10 says, "God, create a pure heart in me, and renew a right attitude within me" (ISV).

How is your heart, your attitude?

Sin interrupts us. Redemption saves us. Restoration returns us. Renewal resumes us.

PRAY

Father, thank You for redemption, restoration, and renewal to live in relationship with You. In Jesus' name, amen.

DAY 52

BEST DAY EVER

Taste and see that the LORD is good. Oh, the joys of those who take refuge in him!

– Psalm 34:8 NLT

What is your best day ever? Has it changed over the years, or is there a moment in time so spectacular nothing else to date has overshadowed it? Your best day ever may be simple or elaborate. Is it the day you or a loved one rang the bell sounding the defeat of cancer? Is it the birth of a child that testing said you could never conceive? Is it the achievement of a long-awaited accomplishment?

Is it any of these?
—A vividly memorable family vacation
—A meticulously planned milestone celebration
—A breathtaking hike at a national park
—An amusement park day of thrill rides
—Your baptism or the baptism of someone you fervently prayed for
—Your wedding (or divorce)
—A day carved out for you, a day of absolute peace and tranquility

My best days have continued to evolve. God's goodness and mercy have shown me that the best is yet to come! Each day and experience is an opportunity for more grace and goodness, an opportunity to share goodness with others so they can enjoy the best days ever.

Reflect on your best day ever. Was it filled with excitement and exuberance or complete peace and serenity? What made the best day ever so special? How did you feel?

No matter what your best day has been thus far, the absolute best day ever will be hearing, "Well done, good and faithful servant" (Matthew 25:23 NIV).

PRAY

Gracious God, thank You for each day. The best is yet to come—spending eternity with You. In Jesus' name, amen.

DAY 53-59

DAYS OF INTENTION

So too, faith, if it does not have works [to back it up], is by itself dead [inoperative and ineffective].

– James 2:17 AMP

The final week of this devotional, there are actions to choose and complete each day.

Stop! Take a moment to call or message someone with words of encouragement. Your contact could be a difference maker. You may need encouragement, but intentionally moving outside your needs to lift another up is gratifying. Over the next week, choose an action each day to complete.

- Read an old love note. Remember how special you are. If there are no love notes to retrieve, read Lamentation 3:22-23, Isaiah 54:10, Psalm 139, and Psalm 91, and feel God's love surround you.
- Give a hand clap of praise to God, for He is so good. Describe how He has been good to you.
- Write down your favorite memory from this week.
- When is the last time you held someone's hand? Well, today is the day. Find a friend, a senior citizen, someone from your church family, or someone ill who needs a human touch.
- Wink at the love of your life.
- Ask for a foot rub. Better yet, give a foot rub. You know, Jesus washed others' feet!
- Relive the moment you proposed or received a proposal.
- Sing your favorite song as if no one else was watching (or listening).
- Ask for forgiveness.
- Offer a smile to everyone you see today—everyone.
- Pray a bold prayer.
- Look in the mirror and say: "God loves you and so do I."
- Write a note or card.
- Make someone laugh.
- Forgive someone (including yourself).
- Look up.
- Bow down before God (literally).

- Share a meal.
- Pray with someone.
- Perform a random act of kindness.
- Express gratitude to someone who has made an impact on your life.
- Take a walk and observe God's creation.
- Give something away.
- Be still and listen. No talking, just listening.
- Share your story (vulnerability required).

Seven Days of Intentional Action

The week has concluded. Did you notice any difference between yourself or others? The difference is your intentionality to share love in word and deed.

Write down the daily action you completed and the result. Describe how you feel.

	Action	Result
Day 53		
Day 54		
Day 55		

Day 56		
Day 57		
Day 58		
Day 59		

PRAY

Lord, help me be intentional about showing Your love. In Jesus' name, amen.

DAY 60

DAY OF ONE HUNDRED "KISSES"

Greet one another with a kiss of love. Peace to all of you who are in Christ.

−1 Peter 5:14 NIV

You have just completed seven days of intentional action. Good news: there is more!

How often do you offer kisses throughout the day? You might count one, two, three, forty-five. But one hundred kisses a day is intentional. I mean intentional! Is it possible or desirable? We will define "kisses" as acts of love and kindness toward others. It could be a combination of smiles, greetings, thoughtful messages, gracious gestures, and acts of kindness toward others. (This does include actual kissing.) What do you think? Can you? Well, I know you can. Will you choose a day to give one hundred kisses? Show care for others. Brighten up the day one hundred times. Someone needs a "kiss" of kindness. Be creative! Time to act. Let the "kissing" begin!

--- **PRAY** ---

Heavenly Father, thank You for Your loving kindness. Help me to show and share that love in abundance. In Jesus' name, amen.

CONCLUSION

It is my prayer that the past sixty days have helped you look within yourself, deepen your relationship with our omnipresent God, and grow closer to others. I hope you have used this book as a tool. That you have highlighted, made notations, and referenced the Scriptures included while humbly sharing your desires and needs with God and those close to you.

Writing this devotional has been cleansing, cathartic, reassuring, and uplifting for me. Thank you for sharing this journey. May God bless you and fill you with His love, grace, and mercy.

In every circumstance, God is present. He loves and welcomes you.

The final two entries are tributes to the twin pillars who anchored the foundation of my faith: my father and mother.

WHO IS A GODLY FATHER?

Fathers, do not provoke your children to anger by the way you treat them. Rather, bring them up with the discipline and instruction that comes from the Lord.

–Ephesians 6:4 NLT

A godly father supports hopes and dreams. He encourages you when you cannot or will not believe in yourself. He is a pillar of strength and a shield of protection. He is a support system and shoulder to cry on. He allows the tears to flow freely but does not allow you to wallow in them endlessly. A father is an accountability partner. He teaches you to be accountable and challenges you to surround yourself with others who will do the same. He sets elevated expectations and standards of measurement. His best lessons are reflective of how he lives.

He is not perfect by any means, but perfect love prevails. A father's love is immovable. No argument, disagreement, anger, failure, or disappointment can separate us from his love. And, if his child is ever separated from him, a father is always there waiting with welcoming arms.

My father was this godly man. He cherished his wife and loved his family. He was a man of unfailing faith: it was and is unshakeable. He was firmly rooted in God's love. And my most treasured lesson is sharing that deep and abiding love of God, love from which all else emanates. It is the greatest gift and testament of his life and love.

---- **PRAY** ----

Thank You, God, for my father. His faith was unshakeable.

WHO IS A GODLY MOTHER?

She opens her mouth with wisdom, and the teaching of kindness is on her tongue. She looks well to the ways of her household, and does not eat the bread of idleness. Her children rise up and call her blessed; her husband also, and he praises her: "Many women have done excellently, but you surpass them all." Charm is deceitful, and beauty is vain, but a woman who fears the LORD is to be praised.

– Proverbs 31:26-30 ESV

A godly mother is love and grace in action. She is kind, considerate, and compassionate. She is stern and a disciplinarian, when needed. She guides and teaches. She nurtures and listens. In my case, she is a woman filled with the love of God. When her faith is under fire and her foundation is rattled, her strength is the wellspring of God. She is a lesson of love.

My mother and father are strong pillars, without whom I could not stand in confidence.

PRAY

Thank you, God, for the woman I am proud to call MOTHER. She walks and talks with you.

www.ingramcontent.com/pod-product-compliance
Lightning Source LLC
Chambersburg PA
CBHW030232100526
44583CB00013BA/888